WHAT'S IT LIKE TO BE ENLIGHTENED?

*A Guide To Your Experience
Of Full Enlightenment*

BOOK I

Deric J. Gorman

Visit us at:
www.whatsitliketobeenlightened.com

Contents

Chapter 1: This Is Enlightenment   1

Section I
Spirit-Based Enlightenment

Chapter 2: Perceiving The Presence Of Spirit   19

Chapter 3: Experiencing Yourself As Spirit   41

Section II
Awareness-Based Enlightenment

Chapter 4: Recognizing The Presence Of Awareness 57

Chapter 5: Knowing Yourself As Awareness   71

Chapter 6: Spirit vs. Awareness   85

Section III
Full Enlightenment

Chapter 7: No-Things And Unbounded Oneness   107

Chapter 8: No-Self And Ultimate Happiness   125

Chapter 9: Spiritual Self Or No-Self?   149

Chapter 1

This Is Enlightenment

Closer Than You Think

Enlightenment is closer than you think. It's always right in front of you. It's inside, above, behind, and all around you too. The entire field of your experience is a field of enlightenment. There is not a single hair, a speck of dust, or a sliver of your experience that is ever outside of enlightenment.

If enlightenment were an ocean, then the objects in your world would be its waves. Waves are not separate from or other than the ocean. They are expressions of it, you could say. Likewise, your everyday world and the things in it are not separate from or other than enlightenment. They are displays or expressions of it.

So despite appearances, you are never actually apart from enlightenment. If you are searching for it, it's right *here*. Even as you look for enlightenment, you always look right at it. It's at once hidden and fully revealed in the very experience you are now having.

The Perfection Of Enlightenment

In enlightenment, everything is perfect exactly as it is. The whole field of experience shines with unwavering perfection. This perfection is fully intact, and it's not created or sustained through any effort of the self. *What is* already is perfect. This perfection is invisible outside of enlightenment. But once you find enlightenment, the natural perfection of all experience becomes visible in an instant.

Is a buttercup a weed or a flower? The answer depends on your perspective. There are many plants that could be considered either weeds or flowers: buttercups, clovers, dandelions, and daisies. Ordinarily, these plants are classified as weeds, and we are oblivious to their manifest beauty. Yet, if you take a moment to notice them, you will recognize how beautiful they really are. In this way, the same plant can be seen as an ugly weed or a beautiful flower, depending on how you look at it.

The same is also true of your life. Is this moment an ugly weed or a beautiful flower? Like the buttercup, clover, dandelion, and daisy, your life doesn't need to be changed in order to become something beautiful. It already is beautiful just as it is. Although this beauty is hidden from you before enlightenment, with an enlightened "perspective" you are able to see it. With enlightenment, a beauty and perfection that never fade become visible in all of life.

The Happiness Of Enlightenment

We all search for happiness, and enlightenment is the culmination of this search. You could say that the happiness of enlightenment is ultimate happiness. It is the greatest and most fundamental happiness there is. It is a happiness within which there is no need for more happiness. And it is a happiness that is intrinsic to all things.

In a way, ultimate happiness is so big that no self can contain it. It can't fit into you any more than the whole ocean can fit into a single fish. Like a fish, you are too small at first. But with enlightenment, you let go of your small self and become inseparable from all of *this* —the whole "ocean" of life. As all of *this*, you are big enough for ultimate happiness, and you realize that it is your nature.

Ultimate happiness is not known outside of enlightenment. Outside of enlightenment, ultimate happiness will always lie beyond your reach. Whatever non-ultimate happiness you find, on some level you will always be left wanting more. Therefore, you will never be able to overcome your unhappiness, unless you find enlightenment.

Your Innermost Experience

We all have an innate need to find enlightenment. There are some of us who not only recognize the need for enlightenment but prioritize it.

At the same time, there is a way in which even now—even outside the enlightened state—you are already in touch with enlightenment. You are already in touch with it on a deeper, non-conscious level. And it is because you are already in touch with it on a deeper, non-conscious level that you seek it out in the first place.

This continuous, deeper connection with enlightenment makes you constantly feel as though there is something else, something different, something better, something more. It engenders your life with an underlying sense of dissatisfaction and incompleteness that nothing seems to take away. And it guarantees that on some level you will always be restless until you rest in enlightenment, having made the enlightened reality that you are already in touch with, on an innermost level, outwardly real for you.

Enlightenment Is Natural

Sooner or later, the reality of enlightenment will become obvious and undeniable to you, as long as you seek it out. Of course, as you begin your spiritual search, enlightenment isn't obvious or undeniable to you yet. Understandably, you might have doubts about whether it exists. Or, even if you believe it exists, you might have doubts about your ability to ever find it. However, it does exist, and—as already explained— there is something deep within all of us that knows it, even if at times this knowing feels faint or far away.

Enlightenment is not a special state reserved for the spiritual elite. Anyone can find it. Furthermore, finding it should not take lifetimes, decades, or even very many years. There is no practical reason for this.

Many of you have already had glimpses of enlightenment at some time in your life, perhaps in childhood. Many people get glimpses of it on their first spiritual retreat, in a single session with a spiritual teacher, or at home just contemplating a spiritual book. Although a fleeting glimpse is not the same as a persistent experience, most people start with glimpses. In time, those glimpses become permanent or stabilize. These sudden glimpses suggest that there is no impenetrable barrier between you and enlightenment. Experiencing it can happen spontaneously, even when you aren't looking for it. And if you do look, you will find it.

Not only should the spiritual search not take long, but it shouldn't be particularly difficult either. Why should it be? There is no reason why the search for enlightenment can't be a relatively easy, even enjoyable process. Remember what your goal is. You aren't trying to master esoteric texts or techniques. You don't have to change your name, adhere to a special diet, or adopt a new lifestyle or culture. You don't need to become a saint (nor will enlightenment make you a saint). You are simply seeking to glimpse what is already here— and what you already know on an innermost level— and you are attempting to make that glimpse stick. The enlightenment you are looking for already dwells within you. So the experience of it is always well within your reach.

Finally, as extraordinary as experiencing enlightenment might sound, it actually becomes quite normal. In time, you adjust to it, as you do anything else. The fact that you experience it ceases to be a big deal. Sooner or later, you will even fail to remember that there was ever a time when you didn't experience it. And, for all practical purposes, you will forget that there is any other way to be.

The Forms Of Enlightenment

As you have no doubt noticed, this book is about

enlightenment. However, it's not about just one form of enlightenment. It's actually about more than one form.

So far, we have touched on what could be called the full or complete form of enlightenment. But there is also another form of enlightenment, a partial or incomplete form. In fact, there are two primary kinds of partial enlightenment. *Section I* explores the first kind of partial enlightenment. *Section II* explores the second kind of partial enlightenment. Finally, *Section III* explores the full form of enlightenment. So, altogether, there are three different "enlightenments" explored in this book—two partial and one full.

The partial or incomplete forms of enlightenment happen to be much more well known and widely experienced than the full form. More than ninety-five percent of the spiritual teachers today teach partial forms of enlightenment. They are not actually offering the full form of enlightenment. As spiritually developed as these teachers may be, generally speaking, they haven't the faintest idea that their form of enlightenment is only a partial form and that an

entirely different form of enlightenment is possible—
the full form.

Unfortunately, the same can be said of their students.
They have no idea that the form of enlightenment that
they are pursuing as students of these teachers is a
partial form rather than the full form. They may be
yearning for the full form, but instead they are seeking
—or, in some cases, experiencing—a partial form
without realizing it. Like their teachers, they can't tell
the difference between the full and partial forms of
enlightenment.

By familiarizing yourself with the different forms of
enlightenment, however, you will be able to
distinguish them from one another. It's very easy to
mistake the experience of partial enlightenment for full
enlightenment. In fact, it's virtually inevitable, unless
you know the difference between them. By the end of
this book, you will be able to recognize the difference
between partial and full enlightenment.

With that said, if what you seek is not full enlightenment but instead one of the partial forms of enlightenment, you are free to do so. You should search for, find, and live out whichever form of enlightenment you consider to be most meaningful and worthwhile. This book will help you to do that, regardless of which form you seek. In the chapters that follow, I attempt to describe each of these forms of enlightenment—both the full *and* the partial forms—in a way that someone who is experiencing them would easily recognize and accept. At no point do I disparage any of them.

At the same time, you shouldn't give your life to a form of enlightenment you don't ultimately want. If you seek full enlightenment, then you don't want to mistake one of the partial forms for the full form. And you don't want to spend the rest of your life in a partial form thinking that you have arrived, when you've only made it partway to the destination you really long to be.

So, if you are seeking enlightenment—whether in a partial or full form—after reading this you will clearly understand what you are looking for and what you should avoid. As a consequence, you will be able to find enlightenment much more easily, quickly, and reliably. I sincerely hope this book helps you on your journey to enlightenment, no matter what form you seek.

What's It Like To Be Enlightened?

Section I

Spirit-Based Enlightenment

What's It Like To Be Enlightened? is about the direct experience of enlightenment. It's about what you actually experience when you are in a state of enlightenment. In what follows, we embark on an experiential exploration of the lived experiences of three different states of enlightenment.

As mentioned in the previous chapter, *Section I* and *Section II* explore two kinds of partial enlightenment. When the word *enlightenment*—or related words such as *awakening* and *realization*—are used today, they almost always refer to one of these two kinds of partial enlightenment. If you are familiar with the contemporary spiritual scene, you will likely have encountered one or both of them before. As you read

15

about them in the next few chapters, you will probably recognize one or both of them.

I should point out that you don't need to fully understand each form of enlightenment before moving on to the next one. Until you are able to experience a particular form of enlightenment, to some degree it will always remain obscure. That is only natural. In time, your own direct experience of enlightenment will reveal all that I've written about it and more to you. So, as you read, don't get hung up on anything that you might not perfectly grasp straightaway.

Also, if you are mainly interested in the full form of enlightenment, then you don't have to fully understand the two partial kinds of enlightenment covered in *Section I* and *Section II* before moving on to *Section III*, where the full form is discussed. A general impression of the two partial kinds of enlightenment should be enough to prevent you from confusing them with the full form, and to enable you to distinguish them from one another.

With that being said, the form of enlightenment we now turn to is the first of the two partial kinds of enlightenment. This kind of enlightenment can be called "spirit-based enlightenment," because it rests on the experience of spirit. Spirit-based enlightenment has two main aspects to it: perceiving the presence of spirit and experiencing yourself as spirit. Chapter 2 is about perceiving the presence of spirit, and Chapter 3 is about experiencing yourself as spirit.

What's It Like To Be Enlightened?

Chapter 2

Perceiving The Presence Of Spirit

What Is Spirit-Based Enlightenment?

Notice what you are perceiving in your experience
now.

What objects are present in your world? What do you
see? When I look around my living room, I see the blue
chair my friend gave me, a laundry basket overflowing
with clothes, and my dog curled up on the floor,
expanding and contracting as she breathes.

What sounds are present in your environment? What do you hear? In this moment, I hear the washing machine in the other room filling with water, I hear the hum of the air conditioner, and I hear the distant roar of a plane flying above.

What sensations are present in your body? What do you feel? Among other things, I feel the pressure of my body against the sofa, a little tension in my neck and shoulders, and a slight weakness in my body which lets me know that my blood sugar is dropping and I'll need to eat soon.

Along with what you are seeing, hearing, and sensing in your physical world, you are also perceiving things in your "mental world" or in your mind. For instance, you might be hearing a voice in your head speaking these words right now as you read them. You might also be experiencing other associated or incidental thoughts competing for your attention.

Besides what you are seeing, hearing, and sensing in your physical world and what you are encountering in your mind, what else are you perceiving in your experience? More specifically, are you also perceiving the presence of spirit? Spirit is just as real and eventually becomes just as obvious to you as anything else that you are now perceiving.

Spirit is ever-present, changeless, and beyond time and space. It is in a permanent state of wellbeing. Spirit is who you fundamentally are. It resides in the heart of all things, and it is the ground of the world. Everything that you are now experiencing is one in spirit. Are you perceiving *this?*

In addition to all that you perceive physically and mentally, the experience of enlightenment simply includes the perception of one more thing: the presence of spirit.

Spirit-Based Enlightenment Defined: Part I

In this and the next chapter, we explore the form of enlightenment that is based on the experience of spirit.

Part of what the experience of spirit consists of is the *perception* of spirit. In fact, this is the first half of our definition of spirit-based enlightenment: it is the ability to consciously perceive the presence of spirit. This is a practical definition. If you can persistently perceive the presence of spirit, then you are enlightened. If you can't, then you are not.

I imagine that for some of you, this definition might seem too straightforward or too black-and-white. However, without the ability to perceive the presence of spirit, you can't function in a spiritually "awakened" way. That is, you can't know yourself as spirit, you can't recognize it in others, you can't behold it in the world, you can't live your life in intimate relation with it, and much more. Everything else rests on your ability to first perceive the presence of spirit. So perceiving it is absolutely necessary. If you are seeking enlightenment, then what you are doing—practically speaking—is attempting to acquire the ability to perceive the presence of spirit.

Understandably, the perception of spirit might seem
unattainable at first, but everyone has the capacity to
perceive it. As incomprehensible as it might seem to be
able to perceive something that is ever-present,
timeless, boundless, and changeless, believe it or not,
perceiving spirit eventually becomes as normal and
natural to you as anything else that you consistently
perceive—your hands, your breath, the objects in the
room, and the empty space around you.

After enlightenment, the presence of spirit becomes
stabilized, and it is always with you. So much so that it
can cause you to almost forget that it is there—much
like the shirt you are now wearing. You won't need to
worry about it or put energy into keeping it around.
You won't lose it and have to go looking for it again.
You won't doubt its existence. Nor will you be in
perpetual awe over the fact that you can experience it.
Believe it or not, this extraordinary spiritual reality can
eventually become a permanent part of your ordinary
reality. Like the shirt that you are wearing, at times you
might even take its presence for granted. This isn't
surprising, as the constant touch of spirit is more

comfortable and familiar to you than that of any shirt
or piece of clothing you could possibly wear.

The Places Spirit Dwells

So, spirit-based enlightenment consists of the ability to
perceive the presence of spirit. In this enlightened state,
there isn't only one place or part of your experience
where you perceive the presence of spirit. There are
many possible places where you can perceive it. Let's
consider the three main places now.

The first and most common place where you perceive
the presence of spirit is *within* yourself. Prior to
enlightenment, when you look within, you encounter
your body sensations, emotions, and thoughts. But in
this enlightened state, when you look within, you also
encounter the presence of spirit dwelling inside you.
Your interior has a new—or, at least, a newly
discovered—presence inside it.

With enlightenment, this presence becomes a permanent part of your overall "anatomy," if you will. In other words, the presence of spirit is always there inside you. It's as constant and accessible to you as your foot, your arm, or any other part of yourself. No effort is required to keep it there. Even though your attention might wander away from it, it never leaves you and you never lose it. The place inside you where spirit dwells is often called your "center," "core," or "heart." Although you are now able to consciously perceive the presence of spirit in your heart, you also recognize that it was always there, even though you couldn't perceive it before.

I should also mention another important aspect of the experience of spirit within. In this experience, you not only encounter the presence of spirit within yourself, but you also experience the presence of spirit *to be* yourself. This presence isn't just *in* the heart of yourself; this presence *is* the heart of who you are. In other words, spirit doesn't just dwell inside you; it *is* you. This is the subject of the next chapter, however, and we explore it more there.

So, in this enlightened state, the most common place to perceive the presence of spirit is within yourself. But there is also a second place: you can perceive the presence of spirit outside of yourself as well. More specifically, you can perceive the presence of spirit within others. In light of the fact that spirit dwells within you, it shouldn't come as a surprise to find out that it dwells within others too. Therefore, with enlightenment, you perceive the presence of spirit not only in your own heart but in the heart of all things.

While this might sound like a nonliteral or even poetic way of speaking, it is not. It describes your actual perception of others in this state of enlightenment. When you look at another person, you see not only their physical form, but also their "spiritual form." You perceive the presence of spirit shining inside them. Therefore, after enlightenment, whenever you are in the presence of another, you also know that you are in the presence of the divine. You are awakened to the divine presence that dwells in the center of everyone and everything.

To be clear, this is true not only of your perception of
other human beings, but also of your perception of all
conscious beings. Furthermore—and this might come
as a surprise—it is also true of your perception of all
non-conscious, insentient, and inanimate things as
well. In this enlightened state, you perceive the
presence of spirit within all things: human and non-
human, conscious and non-conscious, sentient and
insentient, animate and inanimate. It dwells within
your lover, your neighbor, your dog, the shoe, the tea
cup, the wall, the tree, the stream, the mountain, and so
on.

Practically speaking, all of this might not be obvious to
you right away, but sooner or later, you will come to
experience this. Spirit resides not only in your heart,
but also in the hearts of others. It is in the heart of all
things. Most of you will perceive it within yourself at
first. But some of you will perceive it outside of
yourself and within others at first. Nevertheless, any
place that you perceive it is valid. You can perceive it

within yourself, within others, or both. There isn't only one right or authentic place to perceive it.

Before concluding, I should also mention that there is another, third place where you can perceive the presence of spirit. On the surface, this third place might seem similar to the second place, but it is very different. This third place is not exactly "within" yourself or "within" others. Instead, you perceive the presence of spirit as underlying and pervading the world and all things. Unlike the places discussed above, in this third instance the presence of spirit is not exactly encountered *in* the heart of yourself or of others. It is not another part of your inner "anatomy" or that of others. It has no locus or center in anyone or anything. In this third instance, rather than conceiving of spirit as the "heart" or "center" of something, you can simply imagine it as another "layer" or "level" of reality. This level underlies and pervades your entire world. It is not concentrated within or emanating from anything, but it is evenly distributed beneath and throughout all of the world. And it is perceived in and through every part of the world equally.

So, technically speaking, spirit is still in a sense both "within" yourself and "within" others, since it interpenetrates all things. But the difference between this third instance and the first two is that spirit is not localized "within" yourself or "within" others anymore. Instead, its presence is "spread" or uniformly manifest throughout all experience; it equally pervades and underlies all things.

In summary, these are the three main places where you perceive the presence of spirit in this form of enlightenment: within yourself, within others, and beneath/throughout the world. As stated above, each place is valid, and none is inherently better than the others. Wherever you initially perceive it, in time you will likely come to perceive it in multiple places. However, this is not to say that you *must* come to perceive it in more than one place. You can if you want, but that isn't necessary. Doing so won't make your enlightenment more real or complete or authoritative. Wherever you permanently perceive the presence of spirit, that is sufficient.

The World In Enlightenment

So, enlightenment consists of the ability to perceive the presence of spirit—within yourself, within others, and beneath/throughout the world. But how does the perception of spirit impact your reality? More specifically, what happens to your ordinary world in this state of enlightenment? Is it still present? Is it absent? Is it replaced with another more "spiritual" world or reality?

This might come as a surprise, but the ability to perceive the presence of spirit doesn't mean that you cease to perceive your ordinary world. In this form of enlightenment, your ordinary world does not disappear. Your world and the things in it are still present. In fact, nothing about your world or anything in it fundamentally changes. Perhaps a better way of understanding this experience of enlightenment is to think of the presence of spirit as something that is *added to* your current experience of the world, rather than something which takes away your world.

I imagine that this might be contrary to some of your expectations about enlightenment. There are two major reasons for this. The first is that the world actually does disappear—at least, in some sense—in another form of enlightenment—the full form. I discuss the full form of enlightenment in the last section of this book. However, as you are aware, the focus of this section is on a different form of enlightenment—the partial, spirit-based form. And in the spirit-based form of enlightenment, your ordinary experience of the world continues.

Nevertheless, since it is not well understood that there is more than one form of enlightenment, descriptions of the various forms of enlightenment are often confused with one another. In this case, descriptions of full enlightenment, in which the world *does* disappear, are confused with spirit-based enlightenment, in which the world *does not* disappear. However, hopefully this exploration can help to clear up some of this confusion.

The second reason why there is confusion about the world disappearing in spirit-based enlightenment is because even accurate or correct descriptions of it might seem to imply that it disappears. Below are some made-up examples to illustrate this point. These examples represent statements you'll hear uttered about spirit-based enlightenment. Though they are technically correct, these statements are still misleading, as they can easily be misinterpreted as implying the disappearance of the world:

The light of God shines through all things.

The Presence of Spirit fills this room.

When you look out at the world, you merely see things; but I see pristine, limitless Being.

You only see a body. Yet through your body, I see the unfathomable beauty of the Infinite.

The Spirit in me recognizes Itself in you. And It sees Itself everywhere.

In Essence, you and all things are timeless and boundless.

Beneath the incessant change of the world, one unchanging Reality endures.

Whatever happens in the world, you are always companioned by a deeper Presence of perfect peace.

Through the vicissitudes of your life, the bliss of your Divine Self remains untouched and unmoved.

Understandably, most of you would have trouble finding the world you experience anywhere in those statements. When hearing statements like that, it is easy to conclude that enlightenment ends your ordinary world. But that would be a mistake. Your ordinary world is there. Even though it is not being emphasized in statements such as those above, you can be sure that it is still being experienced.

With spirit-based enlightenment, both your ordinary world and spirit are co-present with one another: you experience both time and the timeless, space and the spaceless, change and the changeless, manyness and oneness, your humanity and your divinity, and so forth. In short, although you perceive the presence of spirit, your ordinary world persists.

A More Direct Look At Spirit

We've covered a lot of ground already, but I can say a few more things about spirit that might help you to understand it better. In the process of doing this, I will occasionally use the "G-word" or God. If that makes you squeamish, be patient. In Chapters 4 and 5, we explore another form of enlightenment—one that is based not on the experience of spirit or God but on the experience of awareness. And in the final chapters, we explore a form of enlightenment that is based on neither spirit nor awareness, but on the experience of no-self.

In any case, the experience of enlightenment we've been focused on in this chapter rests on the experience of spirit. Spirit, of course, is a word that you are familiar with. In fact, you were familiar with it long before picking up this book. However, unless you directly experience spirit, the reality that the word encompasses will be unfamiliar to you. So, just in case you don't yet experience spirit, I will tell you a little bit more about it and describe it more directly than I have so far.

Spirit is the part of you that is divine and comes directly from God. When you experience spirit, you experience the presence of your own spirit and your own divinity. You don't merely believe that you have a spirit or imagine that you might be divine or come from God in some way. Instead, the fact that you are spirit and come from God is directly perceived by you.

Furthermore, not only is the presence of spirit *your* inner spirit, but it is also the spirit or presence of *God* within you. In itself, the presence of spirit includes

both your inner spirit and the presence of God.
Through spirit, God is always present within you,
whether or not you realize it. So, when you experience
spirit, you experience not only your own divine spirit,
but also God's presence within you.

With the experience of spirit, then, you not only come
to know the reality that the word *spirit* refers to but you
know the reality that the word *God* refers to as well.
Presumably, you've read or heard things about God.
You've possibly puzzled over the nature of God. You
might've even doubted or rejected the existence of
God. Nonetheless, through the presence of spirit—
which holds both your divine spirit and God's—you
directly perceive the reality of God. You not only know
that God is, but you also have an experience of who or
what God is.

Finally, spirit is not only the part of you that is divine
and comes directly from God; it is that part of all
things. Because the presence of spirit is within all
things, all things are divine and come from God, and
God too is present in all things. Spirit is the place

within where you and God are both eternally present and united with each other. And spirit is also that place where you and all things are eternally united in and with God.

We continue to explore what it means to experience the presence of spirit in the next chapter. If you experience spirit already, this description will be sufficient for you to recognize your experience of it and to know what I refer to when I use the word "spirit." Regardless of whether or not you experience spirit, you can compare what you are learning about it with what you will learn in later chapters about awareness and no-self. It is my hope that you will be able to understand all of these enlightenment experiences better by contrasting them with one another. But for now, let's turn to the second aspect of spirit-based enlightenment: experiencing yourself as the presence of spirit.

What's It Like To Be Enlightened?

What's It Like To Be Enlightened?

Chapter 3

Experiencing Yourself As Spirit

Spirit-Based Enlightenment: Who Are You?

Who are you? How do you experience yourself now, in this very moment?

Are you a body or a mind? Or are you a self who is inhabiting a body/mind?

If you are enlightened, then you will know that who you are isn't limited to your body, your mind, or your ordinary sense of self. Instead, who you are also includes the presence of spirit. You don't merely

42

believe that you are spirit; you directly experience yourself to be spirit, along with all that that entails.

As spirit, you are ever-present, changeless, and beyond space and time. You are in a state of permanent wellbeing. You reside at the heart of all things. You are the ground of the world. And all things are one in you.

However unknown this part of yourself may be to you now, rest assured that the experience of yourself as spirit can eventually become as obvious and real to you as your body, mind, and human self now are.

Your Human Self

Prior to enlightenment, you don't know yourself as spirit or perceive this deeper spiritual level of who you are. You might believe that it exists, deny its existence, or be agnostic about its existence. You might have other beliefs about it. Nonetheless, you don't yet directly experience it for yourself.

On the other hand, you do experience your ordinary human self. You might not reflect very much on the question "Who am I?" And you might not have an answer for it. But, you do function as though your human self is real. Furthermore, on a basic level, you also function as though you are that human self—a human body and/or a mind or someone inside a human body/mind.

Yet, with enlightenment comes a fundamental change in how you experience and understand yourself. You are not just able to perceive the presence of spirit—as discussed in the last chapter—but you now also know yourself *to be* spirit.

You Are Spirit

In the enlightened state, if the question "Who am I?" were posed to you, you could easily answer it. You might not use this exact phrase, but your answer would express something like this: "I am spirit: ever-present, changeless, fundamentally one, beyond space and time, and in a state of permanent wellbeing."

If instead of "spirit," you call the deeper spiritual level of what you are "presence," for instance, then you would answer, "I am presence." Or, if you call the deeper level of what you are "the divine," or "essence," or "the heart," then you'd answer, "I am the divine," or "I am essence," or "I am the heart," and so forth. These are all variations of the same answer.

Now, to be honest, you might not actually say any of that out loud. And you might not want to. Depending on the circumstances, that could obviously get a little weird. At the same time, such statements would reflect your deepest truth and reality, and you will likely feel compelled to share this at some time and in some way that feels appropriate.

Regardless of when or how you share this, the point is that with enlightenment, you know this to be your deepest truth and reality. This isn't a thought or a belief that you have about what might be real or who you might be. This is how you actually experience yourself. This is an obvious and undeniable fact that you are directly aware of in an irreversible, ongoing way.

You are ever-present and unchanging. You are beyond space and time. You are the ground of the world and the heart of all things. You are in a state of unceasing wellbeing. And all things are one in you. If this sounds wild or incredible to you now, it actually isn't. Believe it or not, this eventually becomes very ordinary. Although, admittedly, it can take some time to adjust to.

Finally, although who or what you are as spirit might seem mysterious to you now, believe it or not, your ordinary human self is just as much if not more of a mystery. In fact, once you come to experience the presence of spirit, you will know what spirit is. But even then, the exact nature of your human self will remain hidden. Even after enlightenment, though the nature of spirit is known to you, the nature of your human self will still be a mystery. This mystery will remain until the self is gone, which occurs in the full form of enlightenment discussed in the final chapters of this book.

Spirit-Based Enlightenment Defined: Part II

Prior to enlightenment, you don't yet know yourself as spirit. However, you do experience yourself as a human self. In the enlightened state, you don't only perceive the presence of spirit; you also know yourself to be spirit. With that, we can now add the second and final part to the definition of spirit-based enlightenment introduced in the last chapter: enlightenment is the irreversible, ongoing experience of yourself *as* spirit—ever-present, changeless, beyond space and time, and in a state of permanent wellbeing.

All forms of enlightenment entail a fundamental change in how you experience and understand who or what you are. The focus of this chapter (along with the previous one) is on one of the most common forms of enlightenment—spirit-based enlightenment. But, in the next two sections, we explore other forms of enlightenment and other ways in which your experience of self can be fundamentally changed on your spiritual journey. And in the latter section, we explore the type of enlightenment that is characterized by no-self or the absence of self.

The Divine Self

The experience of oneself as spirit is often referred to as the experience of your *divine self*. And your divine self is often contrasted with your human self. Let's examine this contrast in a bit more detail.

Your human self is continuously changing: your thoughts, emotions, and body continuously change. Change on each level of your human self is easily observable over your lifetime. And if you look carefully, you'll also notice that change is occurring moment-to-moment without interruption—both in your mind/body and in the world around you. In contrast, your divine self is unchanging, and its inherent wellbeing—peace, love, tranquility, stillness, silence, and what have you—is constant.

So, for instance, you might be thinking true or false thoughts, kind or unkind thoughts, a lot of thoughts or no thoughts. But, despite what you are thinking, your divine self is unchanged, and its wellbeing persists.

Similarly, you might be feeling "positive" or "negative" emotions—emotions that you like or dislike. You might be joyous, sad, angry, or fearful. But, despite what you are feeling, your divine self is unchanged, and its wellbeing persists.

Your body might be in a state of ease or disease. You might be tired or well-rested, hungry or satiated, healthy or sick, in pleasure or pain. But, despite the state of your body, your divine self is unchanged, and its wellbeing persists.

Finally, the world might be in a state of peace or war, harmony or disharmony, order or chaos. But, despite the fluctuating state of the world, your divine self is unchanged, and its wellbeing persists.

Therefore, whatever is happening in your mind, emotions, body, and in the world, on a deeper level you are completely untouched and unaffected. You, as your divine self, are in a state of permanent wellbeing, and that never changes. What this means, practically, is that the experience of divine wellbeing is always present and available to you. And nothing in your mind, emotions, body, or in the world can alter or reverse that.

The Paradox Of Who You Are

In light of this new, spiritual way of experiencing yourself, your human self is sometimes seen as a "false" or "lower" self, while your divine self is considered the "real" or "higher" self. So, in such a case, if we return to the question "Who am I?" from earlier, a more complete response to that question would be: "I am spirit; but I am *not* a human self." In this instance, you affirm the reality of yourself as a "divine self" or "spirit," but deny the reality of yourself as human.

In spirit-based enlightenment, however, this is not your only option. You can also affirm the reality of yourself as both a "divine self" or "spirit" *and* as a human. So, in response to the question "Who am I?" your full answer would be "I am *both* spirit and mind/body" or "I am *both* my divine self and my human self."

You are free to choose either option—either affirming or denying the reality of your human self. However, with this form of enlightenment, I must emphasize that affirming the reality of both your humanity and your divinity is the more honest and fitting option. Experiencing yourself as divine doesn't mean that you no longer experience yourself as human. The presence of spirit doesn't remove the presence of the human self. Both remain and both are part of your total experience of who you are.

As discussed in the last chapter, we often think of spirit as somehow removing our ordinary world and human self. While this is true for the full form of enlightenment, which is discussed in the final section, in this instance, it is more accurate to think of your ordinary world and human self as being enhanced or having another "dimension" added to them. So, it is not that you lose your ordinary world and human self; instead, you gain another dimension of world and self in spirit.

For some, this might initially seem like a contradiction. How can you be both physical/mental and spiritual, human and divine, finite and infinite, changing and unchanging, and so forth? In truth, these two dimensions or levels of yourself are not opposed or in contradiction with one another. Rather than contradiction, *paradox* is a better word and a better way of understanding who you are in this enlightened state. Both the human and the divine exist within you—and they can coexist harmoniously. Both can be fully embraced by you, and both can be lived deeply and expressed abundantly.

The option that you choose (whether to affirm or deny the reality of your human self and world) will determine the kind of spirituality and life you will live in the years to come. I'll explore more what it means to live an enlightened life in *Book II*. For now, this concludes the main part of our exploration of spirit-based enlightenment. We continue to clarify the nature of spirit-based enlightenment as we contrast it with the next two forms of enlightenment. The form of enlightenment that we now delve into rests not on the experience of spirit but on the experience of awareness.

What's It Like To Be Enlightened?

Section II

Awareness-Based Enlightenment

We now turn to the second of the two partial kinds of enlightenment. This kind of enlightenment can be called "awareness-based enlightenment," because it rests on the experience of awareness. As was the case with spirit-based enlightenment, awareness-based enlightenment also has two main aspects to it: recognizing the presence of awareness and knowing yourself to be awareness. Chapter 4 is about recognizing the presence of awareness, and Chapter 5 is about knowing yourself as awareness.

In case it is not obvious, I should emphasize that awareness-based enlightenment is not another stage or version of spirit-based enlightenment. Awareness-based enlightenment and spirit-based enlightenment are fundamentally different and independent from one another. After directly exploring awareness-based enlightenment in Chapters 4 and 5, awareness-based enlightenment and spirit-based enlightenment are contrasted with one another in Chapter 6. In *Section III*, where the full form of enlightenment is discussed, full enlightenment is contrasted with both partial forms of enlightenment.

What's It Like To Be Enlightened?

What's It Like To Be Enlightened?

Chapter 4

Recognizing The Presence
Of Awareness

What Is Awareness-Based Enlightenment?

What are you aware of right now?

What objects are present in your awareness? What do you see in the room that you are in? What do you hear in the space around you? What sensations do you feel in your body? What do you smell or taste?

Along with everything that you are aware of in your physical world—the sights, sounds, smells, tastes, and touches—you can also be aware of things in your "mental world" or in the space of your mind. For instance, you might be hearing a voice in your head speaking these words right now as you read them. You might also be aware of other associated or incidental thoughts competing for your attention.

Besides what you are aware of in your physical and mental worlds, what else are you aware of? More specifically, are you also aware of the presence of awareness itself? Awareness is just as real and eventually becomes just as obvious to you as any of the things that you are now aware of.

Awareness is still, clear, luminous, and always at peace. It is ever-present, changeless, and beyond time and space. It is within all things, and it is the ground of the world. Everything that you are now aware of is one in awareness. Can you recognize *this?*

In addition to all that you are aware of physically and mentally, the experience of enlightenment simply includes the awareness of one more thing: the presence of that which is aware of all of those things; the presence of awareness itself.

Ordinary Awareness Is Extraordinary

Awareness is present in your experience already. But you might not recognize it yet. Perhaps you never tried to recognize it, and it might not have occurred to you to try. However, not only can you be aware of the things that are present in your experience, but you can also recognize the awareness that knows or is aware of the things in your experience.

As you search for the presence of awareness, remember that you aren't searching for something foreign or far away. "Awareness" is already present in your experience as the ordinary awareness by which you know your everyday self, your everyday world, and the everyday things within it. The ordinary awareness that is already here in the very experience that you are having right now is the presence of what you are searching for.

Are you currently aware of your right hand? You probably weren't until I mentioned it. Nevertheless, focus your attention on your right hand for a moment, and become aware of the sensations there. Take a breath or two. Next, redirect your attention to your right foot. Rest your attention on your right foot for a moment, becoming aware of the sensations there. Take another breath or two. Finally, redirect your attention once more—this time to your right cheek. Rest your attention on your right cheek for a moment as you notice the sensations there.

In each of the experiences above—the experience of your right hand, your right foot, and your right cheek —you were experiencing awareness. Without awareness, you could not have been aware of your right hand, your right foot, or your right cheek. Awareness is the part of your experience that is aware. It is the presence of that which is aware. Anytime you are aware of anything, awareness is present. So you experience awareness continuously. However, prior to entering this enlightened state, you simply overlook its presence.

Because awareness is already present as the ordinary awareness of your everyday experience, you might presume that awareness itself is ordinary. But that would be a mistake. For that reason, it can be misleading to state that awareness is the *ordinary* awareness of your everyday experience, even though that is a completely true statement. Although you are already experiencing awareness as ordinary awareness, you don't yet know what awareness is. You don't recognize it for what it truly is. Once you do, you will discover that awareness is quite extraordinary. Even having been forewarned, you will still likely be surprised.

For instance, space and time appear to be fundamental. But awareness is beyond, independent of, and prior to space and time. The world and everything in it comes and goes, appears and disappears, is born and dies. But awareness is constant, unmoved, unborn, and undying. Your body, emotions, and thoughts change, and the world changes. But awareness is changeless and completely unaffected. The content of experience is in perpetual flux. But awareness is still, quiet, clear, luminous, and always at peace. Finally, the universe contains a multitude of things. But awareness is one and undivided in itself, and all things are one in it.

With that being said, however, the central point is still the same: if you are searching for the presence of awareness—as extraordinary as you will eventually discover it to be—the ordinary awareness of your everyday experience is the direct, ever-available entry point to your search.

The Dimension Of Awareness

One of the hidden obstacles in your search for awareness is that you don't normally think of awareness as a unique part of your experience. In other words, you don't think of awareness as a distinct thing.

The practical reason that you don't *think* of it as a distinct thing is because you don't *experience* it as a distinct thing. Instead, you experience it "mixed" or entangled with everything else that is present in your experience. But in your search for awareness, you'll need to "unmix" or disentangle the presence of awareness from everything else that is present in your experience. Doing this enables you to experience it as it is, in and of itself. And to accomplish this, it helps to think of awareness as something distinct right from the beginning.

In the previous section, I asked you to focus your attention on your right hand and to become aware of the sensations there. Did you recognize the presence of awareness in that experience? If not, let's try again. Return your attention to your right hand and become aware of the sensations there once more. Remember, the awareness that enlightenment rests on is ordinary awareness. You now also know that awareness is a distinct part of your experience. In itself, it is distinct from the rest of what is present in your experience. Can you begin to recognize the presence of awareness now?

Tune into ordinary awareness, and see if you can begin to distinguish its presence from everything else that is here.

As you begin exploring your experience in this way, awareness will probably seem to exist in your mind/body or as a property or function of your mind/body. This can be a strong and convincing impression. It will persist until you begin to disentangle awareness from the rest of your experience and encounter it by itself in its unmixed or pure form.

In reality, awareness is not in or of your mind/body. It is not physical or mental in nature in any way. In saying that awareness is a distinct thing, I don't just mean that it is a distinct property or function of the mind/body. I mean that in itself it is distinct from your mind/body. You can think of awareness as occupying its own "dimension" or level of your experience. The level of your experience where awareness resides is prior to or "beneath" your mind/body. And your mind/body appear "on top" of it. Once you experience pure awareness, you will see that awareness is unmistakably distinct from your mind/body. And the impression that you previously had of awareness being in your mind/body or a property or function of your mind/body will evaporate.

Disentangling Awareness

If you fail to recognize the presence of awareness, it is because it is mixed or entangled with the rest of your experience. We can say that everyday experience consists of awareness plus the content of experience— the sights, sounds, body sensations, emotions, thoughts, and other content of your experience. In the experience of your right hand, for example, that experience consists of awareness plus hand sensations —tactile, proprioceptive, interoceptive, and what have you.

Although you always experience awareness, you have only experienced it mixed with the content of your experience and never by itself. In order to recognize its presence for what it is, what you are after is the experience of unmixed, disentangled, or pure awareness. It is in the experience of pure awareness that its true nature is seen.

Trying to recognize the nature of awareness when it is thoroughly mixed with the content of your experience is like being someone who has never tasted water but is trying to find out what it is by drinking coffee. Technically speaking, there is not one sip of coffee in which water is not present. With each sip of coffee, you are therefore experiencing water. However, you can't distinguish the presence of water from all the other flavors in the coffee. You can drink coffee all day for the rest of your life, and you will still never really know what water is. In order to recognize the presence of water and know its nature, you can't drink coffee. You must taste water by itself—in its pure form, unmixed with anything else. Only then will you really know what water is.

It's a similar situation with awareness: awareness is like water, and experience is like coffee. Just as water is present in coffee, awareness is present in experience, but it is mixed with other things—sights, sounds, smells, tastes, touches, body sensations, emotions, and thoughts. With every experience you have, you are also experiencing awareness. But you can't distinguish the presence of awareness from everything else. In order to see awareness, you can't rely on mixed experience. Rather, you must experience awareness by itself—in its pure form, unmixed with anything else. This will reveal its true nature. Unless you can experience awareness unmixed and by itself, its nature will always be elusive to you.

Awareness-Based Enlightenment Defined: Part I

So, if you are on a spiritual path in search of awareness, then what you are trying to do is straightforward, at least in theory. Awareness is always present. Although you don't recognize it, you are already experiencing it. In itself, it is something distinct. Nonetheless, practically speaking, it is mixed or entangled with the rest of your experience. Because of this, you can't clearly see it for what it is. Therefore, you are trying to "unmix" or disentangle awareness from the rest of your experience. When awareness is disentangled and experienced in its pure form, you recognize it for what it is and know its true nature.

The first part of the definition of awareness-based enlightenment, then, is the ability to recognize the presence and nature of awareness. We continue to discuss awareness-based enlightenment in the next chapter as we explore the second part of our definition: knowing yourself as awareness.

What's It Like To Be Enlightened?

Chapter 5

Knowing Yourself As Awareness

Awareness-Based Enlightenment: Who Are You?

Who are you? How do you experience yourself now, in this very moment?

Are you a body or a mind? Or are you a self who is inhabiting a body / mind?

If you are enlightened, then you will know that who you are isn't defined by your body, your mind, or your ordinary sense of self. Instead, who you are is the presence of awareness. You don't merely believe that

74

you are awareness; you directly experience yourself to be awareness, along with all that that entails.

As awareness, you are still, clear, luminous, and always at peace. You are ever-present, changeless, and beyond space and time. You are within all things, and you are the ground of the world. And everything in experience is one in you.

However obscure this fact may be to you now, rest assured that the presence of yourself as awareness can eventually become as obvious and real to you as your body, mind, and ordinary human self now are.

Awareness Is Self-Awareness

Awareness is always present. It is present not only as the ordinary awareness that you have of objects (as explained in the previous chapter), but also as your ordinary self-awareness. Right now, you are. And you know that you are. You are aware of your own existence in an immediate, non-conceptual way. But who or what is it that is aware of your own existence?

As you have already learned, awareness is the part of your experience that is aware. It is the presence of that which is aware. Therefore, anytime you are aware of anything, awareness must be present. This includes being aware of your own existence.

So, in your experience of ordinary self-awareness, you in fact already experience the presence of awareness. As you saw in the previous chapter, without awareness, you could not be aware of your hand, your foot, your cheek, or anything else. Likewise, without awareness, you could not be aware of the presence of yourself. Just as awareness is present in the ordinary awareness that you have of your hand, your foot, and your cheek, awareness is also present in the ordinary awareness that you have of yourself or of the simple fact that you are.

So as you search for the presence of awareness, remember that you aren't searching for something far away or unusual or foreign to you. Instead, awareness is always present in you. It is present in you as the ordinary self-awareness that is here right now—your awareness of the simple fact that you are.

Both Sides And More

Ordinary awareness of things like your hand and ordinary self-awareness both "contain" the very same awareness. "Awareness" is the ordinary awareness that you have of objects, and it is also the ordinary awareness that you have of yourself.

Take a moment to become aware of your right hand. What is the nature of the awareness by virtue of which you are aware of your right hand? Now, take a moment to become aware of the fact that you are. What is the nature of the awareness by virtue of which you are aware of the fact that you are? Each of these questions has the same answer. If you engage with either one of them until you arrive at the answer, you will end up in the same place: unobstructed, ever-pure awareness.

Therefore, if you are searching for awareness, you can initiate your search from either side of experience: the object side or the subject side. In the previous chapter, we focused on the object side. And in this chapter, we are focusing on the subject side. Awareness is equally present on both sides and equally accessible through both. In fact, awareness is equally present in all experience. Awareness pervades your entire mind/body and the entire world. So, strictly speaking, it can be approached and accessed through any part of experience you like.

You Are Awareness

We've established that you are aware of your own existence or of the simple fact that you are. Nonetheless, as you begin your spiritual exploration, you don't yet know who or what you are. You refer to yourself as "I." Yet you don't know who or what "I" is.

At first, you seem to be identical to your mind/body or to a subject who lives inside your mind/body.

However, if you investigate the nature of who you are,
you eventually discover that "I" ultimately refers to
you as awareness. That is, you discover that who or
what you are is awareness. So although you seem to be
your mind/body or a subject within your mind/body,
in truth you are awareness. You are awareness but
don't know it.

Therefore, awareness is not merely present as the
ordinary awareness by which you are aware of
yourself, but it is also present *as* yourself. In other
words, the awareness that is aware of yourself *is*
yourself. However, if you can't yet distinguish yourself
as awareness from the rest of what you take yourself to
be, you won't recognize this fact about what you are.

Your Ordinary Self Is Extraordinary

Awareness is present in your mind/body self but
distinct from it in the same way that awareness is
present in the experience of your hand—or any object
of experience—but distinct from it. Therefore, in

attempting to recognize the fact that what you are is awareness, you are faced with the same fundamental predicament as the one presented in the last chapter: awareness is always present, but you don't notice it or recognize it for what it is.

Since you are awareness, this is true of you. You are always present. You now know that you are. But you don't yet recognize yourself for what you are. You are awareness, but you don't know it because you are unable to distinguish yourself as awareness from everything else that you experience yourself to be—your body, emotions, thoughts, and what have you. Your goal, then, is to experience yourself as awareness in your unmixed or pure form so that you can encounter yourself as you are, in and of yourself. Otherwise, your nature will always be elusive to you, and you will never really know what you truly are.

In the last chapter, it was also explained that awareness is extraordinary. Of course, since you are awareness, that too is also true of you. Space and time appear to be fundamental. But as awareness, you are beyond, independent of, and prior to space and time. The world and everything in it comes and goes, appears and disappears, is born and dies. But as awareness, you are constant, unmoved, unborn, and undying. Your body, emotions, and thoughts change, and the world changes. But as awareness, you are changeless and completely unaffected. The content of experience is in perpetual flux. But as awareness, you are still, quiet, clear, luminous, and always at peace. Finally, the universe contains a multitude of things. But as awareness, you are one and undivided in yourself, and all things are one in you.

Awareness's Self-Disclosure

The mind can't imagine what pure awareness is. In the end, the mind isn't what finds it. Pure awareness is not in the mind's reality. Its "coordinates" are not on the mind's radar. Even if the mind understands that pure awareness exists or is "out there" somewhere, the mind still cannot see the "place" where pure awareness is. If pure awareness doesn't reveal where it is, the mind will never know.

In the end, the mind must surrender in order for pure awareness to reveal itself. Pure awareness doesn't simply show itself to "you," the mind/body self, or shine its light into your world. Rather, in revealing itself, pure awareness replaces your current reality with its own. In this way, the experience of pure awareness is impossible to anticipate.

As pure awareness, you are at the same time both freed from the limitations of your mind/body and merged with the bliss that is inherent in awareness. To be clear, you are instantly freed from all of the limitations of your mind/body—not some of them gradually but the whole of them at once. Prior to being freed of them, these are limitations the extent of which you don't even fully realize are there. Regarding the bliss, it's perhaps like being saturated in a lake of bliss. Except you are that bliss. As awareness, bliss is your nature. You are subsumed in a lake of bliss that you yourself are simultaneously being and enjoying. One of those experiences alone would be impactful. Together, they make pure awareness virtually irresistible, once it is genuinely experienced.

When all is said and done, however, you as awareness are beyond the mind: not beyond the current state of the mind, and not in a more altered or expanded state of mind. You are beyond the mind itself in a way that the mind can't imagine. Beyond the mind, you know what you are. You know what you, unmixed or pure awareness, is. And you know that "place" that the mind cannot see. It is a "place" beyond the edge of the world where only you as awareness are and nothing else can go.

It is the experience of pure awareness that reveals what you are. Until then, you are only known in an "impure" or "mixed" form. Technically speaking, what you are is always fully present. But prior to the experience of pure awareness, you don't recognize yourself for what you are. You don't know yourself as awareness.

With adequate exposure to awareness in its pure form, however, you establish the knowledge of its presence and the fact that you are awareness. You retain this knowledge even when the mind, body, and world are present. The content of experience no longer mixes with awareness and conceals its presence in the way it previously did. In the presence of the mind, body, and world—whatever the content of experience may be— you don't lose awareness or forget its/your nature anymore.

Awareness-Based Enlightenment Defined: Part II

If you are seeking awareness-based enlightenment, then what you are trying to do is distinguish yourself as awareness from the rest of your experience. This will enable you to know yourself as you are and see your real nature. Therefore, enlightenment is not just the recognition of the presence of awareness but the direct experiential knowledge that you are awareness. In *Book II*, we examine other important usages and meanings of the term "awareness" in spiritual thought and practice.

What's It Like To Be Enlightened?

What's It Like To Be Enlightened?

Chapter 6

Spirit vs. Awareness

Spirit vs. Awareness

Some of you might be wondering how the presence of awareness differs from the presence of spirit. In fact, some of you might not only be wondering how they differ, but you might be doubting that they are different. You might even believe that I'm confused and mistaking what is actually only one deeper spiritual reality for two different spiritual realities.

With that being said, if you have no questions about how awareness and spirit differ or if such questions seem too technical for you at this time, you can skip part or all of this chapter. It's not critical that you understand it before moving on to the discussion of full enlightenment in the next section. But for those of you who are onboard, let's have a closer look at awareness and spirit now.

Two "Ultimate" Realities

While it's easy to distinguish the presence of awareness from the presence of spirit in experience, it's extremely difficult to distinguish them conceptually and in language. If you experience them both, you easily recognize that they are two completely different things. But if you haven't experienced either of them, or even if you've only experienced one of them, then you will have a very difficult time telling them apart. In fact, unless you experience both awareness and spirit, you will likely not even know that they both exist.

To begin with, it is generally assumed that there is only one "ultimate spiritual reality" out there for you to

find. What's more, there is nothing in the experience of
either one of these realities that lets you know that the
other one also exists. For instance, you can find and
experience the presence of spirit and still have no clue
about the presence of awareness. You can be fully
established in the experience of spirit, and awareness
can be just as unrecognized, just as "mixed" or
entangled with the content of experience as ever. In
fact, awareness not only *can* be entangled but it *will be.*
It will remain entangled, unless you also undergo a
spiritual process which leads specifically to the
disentanglement and recognition of awareness.
Likewise, you can fully recognize the presence and
nature of awareness and still not even vaguely perceive
the presence of spirit. You can have no clue that spirit
even exists. And spirit will remain unknown to you
unless you also undertake a spiritual path which leads
specifically to the conscious experience of spirit.

So, the first part of the challenge of attempting to tell
the difference between awareness and spirit is simply
understanding that there are two distinct spiritual
realities that you can find and experience. If you

haven't experienced them both, then you likely won't even know that there are two distinct realities to begin with, let alone the fact that they are being confused with each other and need to be distinguished.

Names Of Awareness And Spirit

Another part of the challenge of attempting to tell *awareness* and *spirit* apart is that the two terms are frequently used interchangeably. In fact, you will encounter all of the following terms used interchangeably, especially on the contemporary spiritual scene: awareness, consciousness, presence, spirit, the divine, God, essence, heart, ground, as well as others. They are all used interchangeably as names for the presence of awareness and the presence of spirit.

Now, if you actually experienced pure awareness, I don't think you would call it "God," for example. At least, that certainly wouldn't be your first choice. If you did use the name "God" for awareness, you would use it figuratively and not literally. On the other hand, "awareness" is the perfect name for awareness. Awareness is what is aware. So the term perfectly matches what it is.

Similarly, if you experienced spirit, I don't think you would name it "awareness." Again, that certainly wouldn't be your first choice. However, names such as spirit, the divine, and God fit the presence of spirit perfectly. The presence of spirit is not figuratively but literally spirit, the divine, and God.

In an ideal world, the presence of awareness would only be called *awareness*, and the presence of spirit would only be called *spirit, the divine,* and/or *God.* But this is not what happens. To complicate things, there are also more general terms such as *presence, heart,* and *ground* which in fairness could be used as names for either awareness or spirit. And, as mentioned, they *are* used as names for both. So, because all of these names are used as synonyms for both awareness and spirit, you can't rely on them. The names themselves aren't enough for you to identify awareness and spirit or to distinguish them from one another.

Descriptions Of Awareness And Spirit

If names themselves aren't enough, what about descriptions? If you go beyond the names and look at how awareness and spirit are described, will that help you to identify and distinguish them? Unfortunately, you will run into the same problem with the descriptions. The descriptions of awareness and spirit tend to be very similar, if not identical, and in most cases they are interchangeable as well. This is true even of good descriptions. More often than not, they are ambiguous and open to multiple interpretations.

For instance, you will find that both awareness and spirit are described as being "ever-present" or always present. As a result, finding or having an experience of something that is "ever-present" isn't enough to enable you to identify what it is. Is it spirit or awareness?

Since both are described in this way, you can't know.
You've likely heard statements such as:

What you are looking for is always, already here.
Become aware of that which is always present.
Your enlightened nature is always with you.
Your true self never leaves you.
The reality you seek is ever-present.
What Is always is.

Unfortunately, you can't be sure which spiritual reality
any of these statements is actually pointing you to.
These statements could just as easily be about spirit or
awareness.

This issue comes up not only for the description "ever-
present," but for other well-known, often-used
descriptive terms as well. As you might have noticed,
in the preceding chapters, I stated that both spirit and
awareness are changeless, one, and beyond time and
space. Other terms that are often used are infinite,
boundless, non-separate, undivided, peaceful, blissful,
tranquil, serene, radiant, still, silent, and so forth. Both

awareness and spirit are described with all of these terms. As a result, these descriptive terms aren't enough for you to identify awareness and spirit or distinguish them from one another. So, for example, a teacher could be pointing you to a reality that is described as ever-present, infinite, changeless, peaceful, and radiant, and yet, even knowing all of that, you still would not know if the reality being pointed to is awareness or spirit.

So how do you actually tell awareness and spirit apart? If you are searching for one—or both—what should you look for? If you find one, how can you tell which one you've found? How can you identify it and tell it apart from the other one? As you've seen, names and descriptions usually fall short. Fortunately, there is another way.

The Function Of Awareness

So, the same names get used for both awareness and spirit: awareness, consciousness, presence, spirit, the

divine, God, essence, heart, ground, as well as others.
And the same basic descriptive terms also get used for
both awareness and spirit: ever-present, infinite,
changeless, non-separate, one, undivided, peaceful,
blissful, and so forth. So how do you distinguish
awareness and spirit from one another?

Initially, the best way to do this isn't by focusing on
their names or descriptions, but on their functions.
Focusing on their functions drastically simplifies things
and helps you to distinguish awareness and spirit more
easily and reliably than anything else. In fact, to
distinguish awareness and spirit from one another, you
only need to know the function of one of them:
awareness. Awareness functions in a distinctive way
that spirit does not. Once I point this out to you, it will
be obvious.

So how does awareness function? Awareness functions
as awareness. It is what is aware. If you are aware of
the sensation of your right hand, it is awareness that is
aware of that. If you are aware of anything else, it is
awareness that is aware of that.

Spirit, on the other hand, does not have this function.
Spirit is not the aware aspect or level of your
experience. It is not that by virtue of which you are
aware of your right hand or of anything else in
experience. This is not spirit's purpose or what it does.
Spirit does not function as awareness.

So, this fact alone is all that is needed for you to
distinguish awareness and spirit from each other.
Awareness is the aware aspect or level of experience. It
is that which is aware. And spirit is not.

Therefore, as you search for and come to experience
awareness and/or spirit, remember that both
awareness and spirit will be given many possible
names and described in many possible ways. However,
only one of these two realities will function as
awareness. With that, you now know how to easily tell
the difference between awareness and spirit.

Lastly, I should briefly mention that the same names
(God, awareness, presence, etc.) and descriptive terms

(timeless, boundless, one, blissful, peaceful, and so forth) that are used for both awareness and spirit are also used to describe the reality experienced in full enlightenment. So the same basic problem arises again: since identical names and descriptions are often used for both partial and full enlightenment, how do you tell which one they are referring to? The answer, of course, is that if you are relying on these names and descriptions alone, you can't tell. Nonetheless, after reading about full enlightenment in *Section III*, you will know how to determine this on your own, without relying on the names or generic descriptive terms that you might encounter.

The "I" Of Awareness And The "I" Of Spirit

Not only are awareness and spirit distinct, but the spiritual "self" that you realize in awareness-based enlightenment is also distinct from the spiritual "self" that you realize in spirit-based enlightenment. Let's consider this topic more closely.

As you saw in the previous chapter, what you discover with awareness-based enlightenment is that there is only one "I" or self. Once you see it for what it is, you understand that it's not a mind/body or someone inside a mind/body. Rather, it is awareness. "I" refers to the one and only self that you have: non-mental, non-physical awareness.

This isn't what you discover with spirit-based enlightenment, however. In experiencing yourself as spirit, you don't disentangle the "I" of awareness from the mind/body or from the content of experience. You don't remove or stop experiencing yourself as a human mind/body self either. Instead, with the experience of yourself as spirit, two selves become available: yourself as human mind/body *and* yourself as spirit. Yourself as mind/body was present prior to enlightenment, and it remains after enlightenment. Therefore, what you are isn't found in a deeper spiritual reality alone—in this case, in the presence of spirit. But what you are is found both in a divine spirit and in a human mind/body. You are not merely one or the other; you are both.

Among other things, you could say that spirit is deeper
than your mind/body self. It is the center and ground
of your mind/body self. It is that by virtue of which
you are divine. It is the presence of God within you. It
is also that aspect of yourself in which you and God
and all things are one. However, none of this removes
the human mind/body self, and it doesn't disentangle
the "I" of awareness from the mind/body either.

This difference can be a source of confusion. With
awareness-based enlightenment, you discover the true
nature of "I." You see that "I" is spiritual in nature—it
is awareness—and not physical or mental at all. You
discover that there is only one "I" or one self. And that
"I" or self is not a mind/body or someone inside a
mind/body. It is awareness.

However, with spirit-based enlightenment, the "I" of
awareness is still entangled with the mind/body, and
the ordinary mind/body self is still intact. Instead of
disentangling the "I" of awareness, you become able to
perceive another dimension of yourself: the presence of
spirit. And you realize that you are not only a human

mind/body, but you are spirit too. So in spirit-based enlightenment, you have two selves or a two-level self: a human mental/physical self and a divine spiritual self. What you are is both human and divine in nature, both mind/body and spirit.

Because of this, it is correct to say, "I am *not* mental/physical; I am *just* spiritual," in the case of awareness-based enlightenment. But it is incorrect to say that in the case of spirit-based enlightenment. In spirit-based enlightenment, you would say, "I am *still* mental/physical; but I am now spiritual *too*."

Those who are established in spirit-based enlightenment often suggest that the first statement ("I am *not* mental/physical; I am *just* spiritual") is wrong. The statement is wrong if it rests on the experience of spirit. But it is right if it rests on the experience of awareness.

Similarly, those who are established in awareness-based enlightenment often suggest that the second statement is wrong: "I am *still* mental/physical; but I am now spiritual *too*." That statement is wrong if it rests on the experience of awareness. But it is right if it rests on the experience of spirit.

In both cases, the same basic mistake is being made: the assumption that there is only one possible spiritual "self" for you to realize in enlightenment. It never occurs that each statement could be correct, but for a different spiritual "self" found in a different state of enlightenment. Nevertheless, if it was simply understood that there are distinct spiritual realities (in this case, awareness and spirit) and distinct spiritual selves (yourself as awareness and yourself as both mind/body and spirit), this mistake could be easily avoided.

For those who have found this excruciatingly nuanced or confusing, I can assure you that you don't have to comprehend everything right now. Nonetheless, even if this is not entirely useful to you now, it might become useful at some point in the future.

What's It Like To Be Enlightened?

What's It Like To Be Enlightened?

Section III

Full Enlightenment

In the previous chapters, we explored two partial forms of enlightenment: spirit-based enlightenment and awareness-based enlightenment. We now turn to the full form of enlightenment.

In the full form of enlightenment, the chronic feeling that there is something else, something different, something better, or something more finally goes away. The full form of enlightenment removes the underlying sense of dissatisfaction and incompleteness that nothing else can take away. And it is in the full form of enlightenment where ultimate happiness, unbounded oneness, and the intrinsic beauty and perfection of all things is disclosed.

The full form of enlightenment does not rest on the experience of a deeper spiritual reality, such as spirit or awareness. Instead, in the full form of enlightenment, there is nothing but a spiritual reality, you could say. In full enlightenment, spiritual reality is the only reality that there is. And the mind, body, world, and everything in them—sights, sounds, smells, emotions, thoughts, and so forth—are not other than this spiritual reality.

In connection with this, full enlightenment can also be characterized as two other things: experience in the absence of a self and of objects; or the experience of no-self and of no-objects. For this reason, full enlightenment can seem highly unusual and even counterintuitive at first. So in the next few chapters I will try to make it as relatable and accessible to you as I can. Chapter 7 is about the experience of no-objects and unbounded oneness. Chapter 8 is about the experience of no-self and ultimate happiness. Lastly, I should mention that you don't have to fully grasp everything in Chapter 7 before moving on to Chapter 8.

What's It Like To Be Enlightened?

What's It Like To Be Enlightened?

Chapter 7

No-Objects And Unbounded Oneness

What Is Full Enlightenment?

Notice what is present in your experience now.

What things are present in your world? What do you
see? What sounds are present in your environment?
What do you hear? What sensations are present in your
body? What do you feel?

Along with what you see, hear, and sense in your physical world, what do you experience in your "mental world" or in your mind? What kinds of thoughts or mental phenomena do you notice?

In full enlightenment, everything that you now see, hear, and sense in your physical world and encounter in your mind appears in a radically different way. Your experience continues—seeing, hearing, feeling, thinking, and so forth—but there are no longer any objects in your experience.

So the answer to the question "What is present in your experience now?" is that objectless experience is present. That is to say, experience is occurring, but there are no objects being experienced in it. There is experiencing in the absence of objects.

I imagine this might be a little difficult to get your head around. So let's look more closely at it now.

Understanding Objectless Experience

Without any objects, what's left to experience? In the absence of objects, is it even possible to have an experience? To be sure, experience does continue in the absence of objects. Although, admittedly, it's difficult to imagine what an objectless experience might be like.

Let's first address some of the most frequent misconceptions. To begin with, the experience of no-objects is not "no experience." It's not unconsciousness or some kind of a mental blankness or blackness. Second, the experience of no-objects is also not "one great blooming, buzzing confusion," to borrow a phrase from William James. It doesn't reduce conscious experience to a swirling mass of undifferentiated sensations. And you don't regress to an undeveloped, baby-like state in which you can't function. Finally, no-objects is also not the experience of a visual field flattened into something resembling a two-dimensional plane or a flat surface. As a flat or two-dimensional object is just as much of an object as a three-dimensional one.

One way to think of the experience of no-objects is as the experience of the world you are now having minus the experience of "objectness." In other words, the experience of no-objects isn't the total elimination of everything you now experience as objects. Rather, it is the removal of their objectness. It includes the objects you are now experiencing minus their objectness. So experiencing no-objects doesn't mean that you've somehow gone through your world, gathered up all the objects, and cast them away. The same objects are still there—chairs, dogs, laundry baskets, body sensations, emotions, thoughts, and what have you. However, they are no longer there as objects; they have lost their objectness.

This might come as a surprise, but it's actually not the senses that divide the world into objects. Although it might seem that way, and we tend to assume that. With the experience of no-objects, your senses still function. For example, you can tell the difference between a chair and a dog, a blue chair and a yellow chair, the bark of a dog and the roar of an airplane, and anything else. But what's different is that the world is no longer divided up. You still perceive everything you used to on a sensory level, but those perceptions are no longer perceptions of objects or of a world which contains objects. So, while the chair, the dog, the airplane, and whatever else are still perceived, they are not perceived as objects. What, then, are they perceived as? I answer that more directly in the sections below.

The Ocean Of No-Objects

This is probably a good time to introduce a metaphor. You can think of no-objects as an ocean and the objects in your world as its waves. Waves are not separate from or other than the ocean. Likewise, your everyday world and the objects in it are not separate from or other than no-objects.

Prior to experiencing no-objects, you are like someone searching for the ocean. You see waves, but you can't recognize the ocean which they are appearances of. As a result, you mistakenly believe that waves are separate, independently existing things. However, needless to say, waves are not separate, independently existing things. They are displays or appearances of the ocean, and they have no existence apart from it.

Similarly, as you search for no-objects, you see objects in your world, but you can't recognize the reality of no-objects which they are appearances of. As a result, you mistakenly believe that objects are separate, independently existing things. However, objects are not separate, independently existing things. Like waves on the ocean, objects are appearances of no-objects, and they have no existence apart from no-objects.

Whenever you see a wave, you are encountering the ocean. And whenever you see an object, you are encountering no-objects, whether or not you realize it. Once you recognize the "ocean" of no-objects, all apparent objects lose their objectness. In an instant, you know that they are not separate, independently existing things but are "waves" or appearances of the "ocean" of no-objects. Therefore, as you search for no-objects, imagine the objects in your everyday world as

115

"waves" on the "ocean" of no-objects and not as being separate from or other than it.

Thinking About No-Objects

So far, I've described the experience of no-objects primarily in terms of what it is not—experience in the absence of objects or without objectness. And I've been reluctant to offer a more positive description of the experience, as I am afraid that such a description will end up making "no-objects" seem like it is another object of experience.

This is somewhat inevitable. Your mind will turn no-objects into another object. Your mind will conceive of, imagine, or represent it in some way, thereby turning it into a mental object. This happens more easily if I describe it in positive terms—in terms of what it is. But it will also happen to a lesser extent even if I only describe it in negative terms—in terms of what it is not, as I have done so far.

Strictly speaking, the mind turning no-objects into another object isn't really a problem in and of itself. In fact, it is useful and perhaps even necessary. This is how our minds function, and it is part of the process of not only learning about the concept of no-objects but even of going beyond the mind and coming to directly experience no-objects for yourself. Even though you go beyond the mind to experience no-objects, the mind plays an integral role in getting you there.

What is crucial, however, is that you do not forget that the actual experience of no-objects is not an experience of the object in your mind—the concept, image, or representation. Rather, no-objects is the experience of a reality in which there are no objects and in which there can never be any. No-objects by nature is never another object and can never become one. So remember that the positive description I now offer is never actually a description of an object of any kind.

Unbounded Oneness

So, in the experience of no-objects the senses don't cease functioning, and experience, generally speaking, does not come to an end. Experience continues, and a "world" is still there in some other form. But how does experience continue, and in what form is the "world" still there?

In the experience of no-objects, what you experience appears in a different way. The "world" or field of experience assumes a new shape or form, you might say. As you've seen, this new shape or form is objectless. But, stated positively, this form could also be called unbounded oneness. Terms like "oneness" are used a lot in spirituality. But the oneness of no-objects is different. It has a few unique characteristics which we'll consider now.

First, in the oneness of no-objects, there is nothing other than oneness. There is nothing else outside it or beyond it or in addition to it. There is oneness and oneness alone, and nothing else. Since the oneness of no-objects alone is and there is nothing else, you could say that it is a *total* oneness.

Similarly, the oneness of no-objects doesn't exist in relation to anything else. It is not present within, throughout, or beneath the ordinary world or things in it. This immediately distinguishes it from the oneness experienced in the partial forms of enlightenment discussed in the previous chapters. Instead of being present within, throughout, or beneath the world, the oneness of no-objects actually *is* the world and everything in it. It is what the world and everything in it has become or now is. Actually, this has always been what the world and all things are. But with full enlightenment, this reality is no longer hidden; it becomes visible. Since the oneness of no-objects doesn't exist in relation to anything else, it is a *non-relative* or *absolute* oneness.

Lastly, not only is there nothing outside the oneness of no-objects, but there is nothing else inside it. It doesn't envelope or contain or include other things in itself. It has no parts inside itself either. It isn't made of any other things. So, for example, your car is one thing. But your car is one thing comprised of many things or parts—an engine, tires, brakes, a steering wheel, a radio, a cup holder, etc. On the other hand, the oneness of no-objects has no parts inside it, and it isn't made of any other, smaller things. Since the oneness of no-objects has no parts or anything else inside it, it is an *indivisible* oneness.

So, we can now state positively what the experience of no-objects is. It is the experience of total, absolute, indivisible oneness. However, as you remember, total, absolute, indivisible oneness is not another object that you experience. It is experience in the absence of objects or without objectness.

What About Spirit/Awareness?

Full enlightenment entails a fundamental change in the form or shape your *ordinary* world takes, but what if your world also includes a *non-ordinary* dimension—specifically, one of the deeper spiritual dimensions of the partial enlightenment experiences—spirit or awareness? What happens to these deeper spiritual dimensions in the full enlightenment experience?

In other words, if you were to enter full enlightenment from one of the states of partial enlightenment previously discussed, what would happen to the deeper spiritual reality experienced there? Would it remain? Or would something else happen? Let's take a moment to consider this.

Spirit/Awareness And Full Enlightenment

First, I should clarify that you don't need to pass through a state of partial enlightenment—spirit-based enlightenment, awareness-based enlightenment, or perhaps even some other kind that we haven't discussed—in order to enter the state of full enlightenment. Although this seems to be the route that most take to full enlightenment, it is not necessary for you to first become established in—or even briefly glimpse—a state of partial enlightenment in order to enter full enlightenment. Not everyone in the state of full enlightenment has passed through a state of partial enlightenment, and you don't need to either. And if you aren't first established in a state of partial enlightenment, then the question of what will happen to the deeper spiritual reality that you experience in that state—spirit, awareness, or what have you—is irrelevant, because that reality won't be there for you in the first place.

But if you do become established in a state of partial enlightenment before entering full enlightenment, what will happen to the presence of the deeper spiritual reality that it rests on? The answer to that question is rather simple: it will no longer be present in your experience—it won't be there at all. Nonetheless, if it were to somehow reappear in some way, its status would be no different than that of the chairs, dogs, laundry baskets, or anything else in your experience— it would be just as objectless as anything else. And it wouldn't be any more or less "spiritual" than anything else either.

Now, if you happen to be established in a state of partial enlightenment as you read this, the suggestion that the deeper spiritual reality that you encounter there will be gone might be unthinkable to you. After all, this deeper spiritual reality is literally the core of who you are, the core of all beings and things, and the foundation of your world. It is also so much more. It is an impenetrable silence beneath the cacophony of the world; an immovable stillness within life's vicissitudes; an unshakeable ground beneath life's turbulence. It is the tangible presence of the sacred itself, in its distilled, immaculate form. It is a constant guide, lighting your way. It is an ever-present holy refuge. It is your most meaningful and intimate companion. It is your Beloved, in whose warm embrace you could disappear forever. And it is even more.

Admittedly, whether you are established in a state of partial enlightenment or not, the loss of this deeper spiritual reality might at the very least sound undesirable. Perhaps its apparent undesirability ranks second only to the disappearance of the self, which we discuss in the next chapter. Nevertheless, in truth, the loss of this deeper spiritual reality is not undesirable. Given what was just expressed above—and perhaps also because I'm a romantic—this feels almost blasphemous to say, but your relationship with your Beloved eventually runs its course. Not only does your Beloved—the deeper spiritual reality—go away and your relationship with it end, but you go away or end as well. There is no Beloved, no self, and no relationship in full enlightenment. Yet, believe it or not, the experience of full enlightenment surpasses the partial enlightenment experiences in a way that is initially unimaginable. Either way, if you first become established in a state of partial enlightenment and then move to full enlightenment, the deeper spiritual reality which is uncovered in partial enlightenment will be gone. But you won't miss it. (Honestly, it breaks my heart a bit to say that!)

Full Enlightenment Defined: Part I

As was the case in the previous sections of this book, as well as attempting to describe the experience of enlightenment for you, I will also provide you with a definition of enlightenment—one that is simple and straightforward so that there is as little ambiguity about what it is as possible. The definition of full enlightenment has two parts, corresponding with the two-part definitions of the partial forms of enlightenment from the earlier sections. This will make it easier for you to compare and contrast the three types of enlightenment, if you wish to.

This chapter focuses on the first part of our two-part definition of full enlightenment: it is the experience of no-objects; it is experience without any objects; it is experience divested of its objectness. Stated positively, it is total, absolute, indivisible oneness. Let's explore the second part of the definition of full enlightenment now: the experience of no-self.

What's It Like To Be Enlightened?

Chapter 8

No-Self And Ultimate Happiness

Full Enlightenment: Who Are You?

Who are you? How do you experience yourself now, in this very moment?

Are you a body or a mind? Or are you a self who is inhabiting a body/mind?

If you are in a state of partial enlightenment, then you will find that who you are is not limited to your body, mind, or ordinary sense of self. Instead, who you are also includes the experience of yourself as a deeper spiritual reality—the presence of spirit or the presence of awareness.

However, if you are in the state of full enlightenment, then you will not experience yourself in any of these ways—as a body, mind, spirit, or awareness. In fact, in full enlightenment, there is no "I" or self inside you. And there is also no "I" or self outside you or anywhere else.

Then, who are you?

With full enlightenment, there is no "I" or self to report on. The very premise of the question is wrong; it presupposes that there must be an "I" or a self.

With full enlightenment, the more relevant question is, "Is there an 'I' or a self?" The answer to that question is unequivocally, "No." There is no "I" or self within or anywhere else to be a body, mind, spirit, awareness, or anything else. Full enlightenment is the experience of no-self or experience in the absence of a self.

As strange as it might initially seem, the experience of
no-self can eventually become even more obvious,
natural, and real to you than any experience of self you
could have.

Understanding Selfless Experience

As mentioned in the last chapter, the experience of no-
objects can be difficult to imagine. But the experience of
no-self is perhaps the most difficult to imagine. In
addition to being difficult to imagine, the notion of no-
self is also counterintuitive. It might sound strange to
suggest that there are fundamentally no objects in the
world, but your mind could at least entertain
possibilities as to what that might mean. However, the
suggestion that there is no self seems to be in direct
contradiction with the most central and persistent
feature of your experience: the fact that you are. In the
absence of yourself, it seems as though there would be
nothing else. You would end, your experience of the
world would end, and all conscious experience would
come to an end as well. In a technical sense, that is all

true. You do end, the world as you experience it ends, and the mode of consciousness that you are accustomed to also ends. However, expressing it in this way can be very misleading. So, in an attempt to avoid this, let's look deeper at the experience of no-self.

No-Self And Consciousness

It's hard to imagine how you could experience anything without a self, not to mention how you would function. Nonetheless, experience continues without a self and so does functioning.

Part of the difficulty in understanding no-self is that you likely confuse consciousness with self-consciousness. But the two are distinct. And it is possible to have consciousness without having self-consciousness.

One way of understanding this is by pointing out the fact that you easily recognize this possibility with animals. Generally speaking, animals are conscious but they are not self-conscious, with a few exceptions. That is, animals don't have a self. Yet they have conscious experiences and function perfectly well in their environments. So, although you might initially imagine no-self as a non-conscious and non-functional state, this is a mistake. The conscious experiences and functioning of animals demonstrate this.

To be clear, I'm not suggesting that the human experience of no-self is equivalent to animal consciousness. Since I am human, I have no way of really knowing what animal consciousness is. I'm just citing animal consciousness to establish that consciousness can occur in the absence of self-consciousness and also that it can be a functional state.

So, no-self is a form of human consciousness. It is a form of human consciousness in which there is no self; it is human consciousness without self-consciousness. I should also mention, as you saw in the previous chapter, that it is human consciousness without consciousness of objects. This includes even the absence of an objective world "out there." Yet it is a perfectly functional form of consciousness.

No-Self And Death

Not only might you confuse consciousness with self-consciousness, but you also might confuse experiencing itself with being a self. In other words, you might believe that the ability to have experiences at all depends on the existence of a self. But the two—self and experience—are distinct. And it is possible to have experiences without having or being a self

For that reason, you might expect that in the absence of a self or of "me," there would be no experience at all. This is what you might even presume death to be. In death, "I" end or die. And because there can be no experience without "me," then when "I" die, experience dies with me. Death is the end of "me" and therefore the end of experience. Or so one might suppose.

However, this is not what's revealed in the experience of no-self. No-self isn't the end of consciousness or experience. A self is not required for there to be consciousness or experience. And the self can "die" without consciousness or experience also ending. The "death" of the self is not biological death or the end of consciousness or experience.

Now, if you do equate death with the end of all experience, when you imagine death you might still picture it in some way. You might imagine death as a cold, unconscious blackness, or as an infinite space devoid of anything, or as being a disembodied point of consciousness floating in nothingness, or what have you. This, of course, wouldn't be the actual end of experience but just another type of experience. Yet it is perhaps the best the mind can conjure up. Nonetheless, to be clear, this too has nothing to do with no-self. No-self isn't an unconscious blackness, or an infinite empty space, or the state of being a disembodied point of consciousness, or anything like that.

If, on the other hand, you believe that the self will continue on in some other form after physical death, then you won't associate death with the cessation of experience. You will associate it with a change in experience or with the ushering in of a different kind of experience, whatever you imagine the afterlife to consist of. In that case, death is not the end of the self, it's the moving on of the self in some other form. So it is also the continuation of experience in another form. Nonetheless, in this instance, you will still be making the same fundamental mistake as those who imagine no-self to be the cessation of all experience—the mistake that a self is required for there to be experience in the first place. This means that, if there is an afterlife, a self won't need to go there or be required in order to experience it.

No-Self And The Body, Mind, And Human Nature

Not only is no-self not the end of consciousness, experience, or biological life, it's also not the end of your human nature. In the experience of no-self, your human nature is preserved. Your mind/body doesn't cease to be a human mind/body. On a bodily level, you still naturally prefer pleasure over pain, being comfortable over being uncomfortable, eating over starving, health over sickness, surviving over dying, and so forth. None of these natural human preferences make you unenlightened, nor do they go away with no-self or in full enlightenment.

On a more mental or psychological level, you still naturally prefer equanimity over anxiety, connection over loneliness, happiness over depression, love over heartbreak, and so on. Not only that, but you still have your personality—for better and for worse—with all of your likes and dislikes. If you liked Italian food when you had a self, you will probably still like Italian food in the absence of your self. If blue was your favorite color, it will probably still be your favorite color. If you had no interest in exotic cars, you will probably still have no interest in exotic cars. You will still have a personality, and it will most likely be basically the same.

Finally, in addition to still having a personality, you will still have your psychological conditioning and wounding. This might be unwelcome news, but the removal of self doesn't remove your psychological conditioning or heal your psychological wounds. This is a big topic, and I discuss it further in *Book II*. But for the time being, don't imagine an "enlightened person" as someone who has zero psychological conditioning or wounding. That person doesn't exist. Becoming enlightened—in either a partial or full form—won't change that for you.

No Self "Inside" Experience

So with no-self, consciousness, experience, biological life, human nature, and the mind/body carry on much like before. But something is nonetheless different— radically different. If no-self is not the end of consciousness, experience, biological life, human nature, or the mind/body, then what exactly is it the end of?

A simple way to put it is that with no-self, there is no longer a self at the center of any of those things. Experience continues, but there is no self "inside" experience anymore. There is no self who is the experiencer of what's happening. There is no self looking out at the world—or hearing, smelling, tasting, or touching the world. There is no self who is thinking thoughts, feeling emotions, or sensing body sensations. And there is also no self upon whom experience is converging or who experience is happening to.

Additionally, there is no self who is the owner of experience: "This is my body, my emotions, my thoughts," or even "my first-person perspective." There is no self who is the author or agent of action: "This is my action. I am authoring and doing this." And there is no self in relationship. In fact, there is no relationship. As no-self is also no-objects—no things, no others, no objective world.

In this way, no-self and no-objects are different terms for one and the same experience. They are different ways of labeling and thinking about it. I'm using these different terms, and approaching full enlightenment from different angles, in the hope that it will help you to understand it better. But either term by itself would suffice, as they both ultimately mean the same thing. So, since no-self is also no-objects, everything that was said about the experience of no-objects in the previous chapter is also true of no-self.

Self-Presence And No-Self

Let's examine what no-self is on an even subtler level now. One way that you know or are aware of yourself is through the act of self-reflection. A well-known example of reflecting on yourself is asking yourself the question "Who am I?" You may or may not reflect very much on this question, and you may or may not have an answer for it. If you were to reflect on it, you might have no idea where to begin or even draw a blank. But you could nonetheless engage in the act of reflecting. You can reflect on who or what you are, whether or not you come up with an answer. And you can entertain possible answers, even if you ultimately don't accept any of them.

In addition to asking yourself "Who am I?" or reflecting on *who* or *what* you are, you can also engage in an even more basic kind of reflection. You can reflect on the simple fact *that* you are. You might think about, puzzle over, dwell on, and contemplate the sheer fact that you are. You normally don't do this. You take the fact that you are for granted. Even though it is such a central, defining feature of your conscious experience (and perhaps because of this), you rarely reflect on the fact that you are. Nonetheless, you can reflect on this fact. You can make your existence an object of your reflection and become explicitly aware of the fact that you are.

So, you can reflect on who or what you are or on the simple fact that you are. These are two examples of self-reflection, and reflection is one way that you can know or be aware of yourself.

With the experience of no-self, however, the self and any aspect of the self known through reflection is gone. You don't reflect on who you are or on your existence for two reasons. First, you no longer are or have an existence to reflect on. There is no one or nothing there existing "inside" you. So you can't make yourself or your existence an object of reflection because there is no self or existence there to be made into an object of reflection—not a physical, mental, or spiritual self or existence. Second, and even more surprising, with the experience of no-self the act or process of reflection subsides. Reflection is no longer a means by which you know your experience. And reflection is not the means by which no-self or the full enlightenment experience is known.

So, any self or aspect of self that can be an object of reflection is absent in no-self, and the act or process of reflection also ceases. But what's more, there is another aspect of self which isn't an object of reflection and can never be an object of reflection that is also absent in no-self. Though this aspect of self can never be made into an object of reflection or experience, it is always there.

141

It's like the background hum of your home that you
don't notice until the electricity goes out and
everything becomes quiet. But this aspect of self is like
the background hum of your whole life—perhaps ever
since your self came online at around fourteen months
old. It is the constant hum of the unseen presence of
self that can never be captured by reflection. And like
the background hum of your home which becomes
noticeable in its absence—once the electricity goes out
—this "hum" of self goes undetected until the self
"goes out," at which point you become aware that it
was there all along.

What is unforeseen and even more unusual about the
experience of no-self is this background "hum" or self
going away. It was not even something you ever
considered could go away, as you had no idea it was
there. It was the background of your whole life and a
constant feature of your conscious experience without
you ever knowing it. Then suddenly it's gone, and by
its absence you instantly realize that it had been there
all the time. So no-self is the absence not only of the self

you know but also of a self you never even knew was there.

No-Self And Depersonalization

In case there is any confusion, I should clarify that the experience of no-self is not depersonalization. It is not the experience of alienation from yourself or the experience that you are unreal. In the experience of no-self, you are not detached from yourself or disconnected from your body sensations, feelings, thoughts, or actions. And you are not separate from yourself, as though observing yourself from the outside.

No-self is the absence of self, not the presence of an unreal self. And it is not detachment or alienation. On the contrary, it is arguably an even more intimate way of experiencing reality. In the experience of no-self, there is no longer a self that is mediating experience. Experience is no longer filtered through a self-other, subject-object structure, so it is known in a more direct, non-dual way. (If you are interested, non-duality is a topic covered in *Book II*.) If anything, you might argue that it is the self which is actually "detached" or at least a step removed from this more fundamental intimacy with what is.

I should also mention that no-objects isn't derealization or the experience that the outside world is unreal. It's not the experience of being detached or disconnected from the world. In the experience of no-objects, there is no outside world whose reality is in question or which you can detach or disconnect from.

No-objects is the absence of objects, not the presence of unreal objects or the presence of an unreal outside world. As explained in the previous chapter, in the experience of no-objects the world takes on another form—an objectless form. The world is not experienced in a detached way but in a new way that is arguably more direct and intimate than our ordinary, objective way of experiencing it.

The Happiness Of No-Self

Not only is no-self not a mental disorder like depersonalization or derealization, but there is a kind of happiness experienced in no-self which is not found or known outside it.

To begin with, you could say that the happiness experienced in no-self is ultimate happiness. It is both the greatest and the most fundamental happiness that there is. It is the greatest because it is a happiness within which there is no possibility of or need for more happiness. It is the most fundamental happiness because it is intrinsic to all things.

This happiness is not localized within a body, mind, spirit, or awareness. The happiness of no-self is not a mind/body happiness or wellbeing. And it's not the permanent wellbeing of spirit or of awareness, which you would know continuously if you were in a state of partial enlightenment. Instead of being localized, the happiness of no-self is at once everywhere and in everything.

In addition to this, the happiness experienced in no-self is already complete and self-sustaining. You don't have to bring it into existence or fashion it. You also don't have to monitor it in order to sustain it at a certain level or manage it in any way. In the absence of self, this happiness is discovered to already be in all experience, and you don't have to do anything for it to be this way.

The happiness of no-self can also be called "pure" happiness. It is pure because it alone is, and it is uncontaminated with anything else. It isn't tainted by things that you might consider unhappy or undesirable such as sadness, fear, anger, ugliness, or ignorance. In fact, it isn't even tainted by things that you would consider happy or desirable such as joy, safety, pleasure, beauty, or knowledge. Actually, pure happiness is the true nature of all of those things—joy and sadness; safety and fear; beauty and ugliness; knowledge and ignorance; and so forth. There is nothing that is an exception to this. Pure happiness is the nature of experience itself.

Finally, I should emphasize that the happiness experienced in no-self is also a non-relative happiness. It doesn't exist in connection with unhappiness. It is never touched by unhappiness. It can't become unhappy or be made less happy. In fact, it doesn't change. So, it's not like a happy feeling that you could have more or less of or that can come or go. It's also not to be mistaken for the greatest amount of relative happiness one can experience. It's not part of a happiness-unhappiness continuum. It's an unchanging, non-relative happiness. So, in brief, the happiness of no-self is an ultimate, self-sustaining, pure, unchanging happiness.

No-Self Is Ultimate Happiness

When the self is present, this ultimate, self-sustaining, pure, unchanging happiness is hidden. On the other hand, when the self is absent, this ultimate happiness appears. Though the self longs for ultimate happiness, it unknowingly hides it from itself. Since it is the very self itself which hides ultimate happiness, the self can look for it forever but will never find it. The self can experience non-ultimate happiness in endless forms. But those endless forms of non-ultimate happiness will always be less or other than ultimate happiness. There are an unlimited number of possible experiences available to the self. But those unlimited experiences will always be something other than ultimate happiness.

To be clear, this is not to say that the non-ultimate kinds of happiness that the self experiences are not important or worth pursuing. Even in the absence of self, pleasure is generally preferable to pain, eating preferable to starving, connection preferable to loneliness, surviving preferable to prematurely dying, etc. It is just that you will never find the ultimate happiness that you long for—and which you intuitively know exists—so long as the self remains. Whatever non-ultimate happiness the self finds, on some level the self will always be left wanting more. So you can never fully go beyond your unhappiness unless you also go beyond the self. In the end, no-self is the final or ultimate happiness that the self longs for.

Full Enlightenment Defined: Part II

This chapter focuses on the second part of our two-part definition of full enlightenment: it is the experience of no-self; it is experience in the absence of a self of any kind—physical, mental, or spiritual. Stated positively, it is an ultimate, self-sustaining, pure, unchanging happiness.

Chapter 9

Spiritual Self Or No-Self?

Spiritual Self vs. No-Self

The most frequent source of confusion in trying to differentiate full enlightenment from the spirit-based or awareness-based forms of enlightenment is the self. In particular, it concerns what exactly constitutes the experience of no-self. Those who are familiar with the spirit-based or awareness-based forms of enlightenment—either conceptually or in experience—often mistake them for the experience of no-self. So before ending, perhaps I should mention a few things that might help you avoid this mistake.

As mentioned in the earlier chapters, you don't need to pass through another form of enlightenment in order to enter the state of full enlightenment. You don't have to become established in the spirit-based form of enlightenment, the awareness-based form of enlightenment, or any other form of enlightenment to enter into full enlightenment. First being in another state of enlightenment for whatever length of time is not a prerequisite to entering into the state of full enlightenment.

However, as you also know by now, if you find yourself in either the spirit-based or awareness-based form of enlightenment, you will both perceive a deeper spiritual reality and experience yourself as that reality. Nevertheless, if you enter full enlightenment from one of these other enlightened states, the deeper spiritual reality that they rest on will disappear. In full enlightenment, you no longer perceive its presence or experience yourself as it. Therefore, full enlightenment isn't the experience of a spiritual self of any kind—a self that is divine, spirit, awareness, presence, essence, etc. Instead, full enlightenment is experience in the absence of a self, experience without a self, or the experience of no-self.

So if the question "Who am I?" were posed to you in the state of full enlightenment, your answer would be "No one" or "There is no 'I'" or "Experience is occurring, but there is no self who is experiencing it." As you can see, this is a completely different answer to the ones given for the partial forms of enlightenment discussed. In response to the question "Who am I?" those forms of enlightenment include statements such as "I am spirit," "I am awareness," and "I am presence." There is an "I" and there is something that it is: spirit, awareness, presence, essence, the heart, etc. But in full enlightenment, there is no "I" and, as you saw in Chapter 7, there is also nothing else for it to possibly be.

In the experience of a spiritual self, there is still a self present. This can be a confusing point. Many mistake the spiritual self of both the spirit-based and awareness-based forms of enlightenment to be no-self.

This is true in one sense. It's not an ordinary human self or an "ego" self, so by contrast it can seem selfless, especially at first. But it is not. It's not even almost or partly selfless. In both the spirit-based and awareness-based forms of enlightenment, the self is still fully intact and functional, whether or not you realize it or want to acknowledge it.

The statements "There is no 'I'" and "Experience is occurring, but there is no self who is experiencing it" are not equivalent to statements such as "I am spirit," "I am awareness," and "I am presence." Previously, you might have mistaken them to be the same basic statement expressed in different ways. But hopefully you are now beginning to recognize this mistake. A self that is a deeper spiritual reality is not the same as no-self. And experience which is occurring in the absence of a self is not the same as experience which is occurring in the presence of a self that is spirit or awareness.

Trying to comprehend the experience of no-self prior to experiencing it is challenging for two main reasons.

The first part of the challenge is that what it means to have no self is impossible to imagine from the point of view of a self. It doesn't matter if the self trying to imagine no-self is in a state of partial enlightenment or not. No-self is equally unimaginable from the points of view of the body, mind, spirit, and awareness.

The second part of the challenge is that the presence of the self is impossible for the self to see. The self is invisible from the point of view of itself. It doesn't matter if the self trying to see or detect itself is in a state of partial enlightenment or not. The presence of the self is invisible from the points of view of the body, mind, spirit, awareness, and whatever else the self might take itself to be.

As a result, it's easy to conclude that the self is gone when its presence is never clearly seen to begin with. While the self is present, you can't clearly see it, and as a consequence you can't really tell if it's there or not. Therefore, you don't actually know what it is that is supposed to be absent or no longer there in no-self. And you won't really know until the self is gone. So the nature of both the presence and the absence of the self will remain elusive until it's gone.

One thing to look out for that will help you recognize the experience of no-self is that no-self isn't exactly something that happens to you. It happens to all experience, you might say. It's not just that you lose your self; all experience loses the self. You never realized that all experience had a self. But when the self is gone, you recognize that the presence of the self wasn't just there, where you experienced yourself to be —in the body, mind, spirit, or awareness. Rather, its reach extended throughout all of your experience. The whole field of experience and everything in it was caught up in and shaped by the self. So when you lose your self, everything else loses it too. Not just you but the whole field of experience and everything in it will be selfless. I imagine that this might sound strange. However, even a temporary taste of the experience of no-self will make this evident for you. Until then, you can keep it in the back of your mind as a way of helping you determine whether or not you are having an authentic no-self experience.

So, the experience of no-self does not take place here in a mind/body. Nor does it take place in spirit or in awareness. The experience of no-self is not known in the place that the self currently seems to be. Rather, no-self is experienced everywhere and in everything. No-self is in the chair you are sitting on, it is in your dog, it is in your right hand, it is in the thoughts continuously appearing and disappearing in your mind, it is in the roar of the plane flying overhead. It is not only *in* those things but it *is* them. No-self is what they are discovered to be.

Back Where We Started

You may not understand everything that you've read in this book, and you don't have to. My primary aim is for you to know that there are different forms of enlightenment, and that there is both a full form and partial forms of enlightenment. If you know that, then I am grateful.

The partial forms of enlightenment are based on the persistent experience of a deeper spiritual reality of some kind, such as spirit or awareness. This deeper spiritual reality is an aspect, level, or dimension of your overall experience. The other aspects, levels, or dimensions of your experience—the sights, sounds, smells, emotions, thoughts, and so forth—exist alongside and in relation to that.

However, with the full form of enlightenment, there is nothing but a spiritual reality. There is no other aspect, level, or dimension of experience. In full enlightenment, spiritual reality is the only reality that there is, and there is nothing else existing alongside or in relation to it.

The mind, body, world, and everything in them—sights, sounds, smells, emotions, thoughts, and so forth—reveal this spiritual reality at all times. This means that everything that is present in your experience right now is revealing this reality to you. The entire field of your experience is a field of enlightenment. So, if you are searching for enlightenment, remember that it is always right in front of you. *This* is enlightenment.

Of course, there is always more that can be said. And there is always much more that will be revealed in the living of enlightenment, if you choose to seek it out. *Book II* will continue to explore the experience of full enlightenment and related topics—unity, oneness, non-duality, awareness, attention, happiness, and more. I hope to see you there.

What's It Like To Be Enlightened?

What's It Like To Be Enlightened?

What's It Like To Be Enlightened?

What's It Like To Be Enlightened?

Acknowledgements

There are many people in my life who I could express gratitude for. However, there are a handful who offered direct support of one kind or another for this book. They are Heather (my wife), Adam and Bridget Jewel, J.R. Evans, Richard McGraw, and Sean Monahan. I want to acknowledge your generosity and let you know that your support was felt and appreciated.

What's It Like To Be Enlightened?

What's It Like To Be Enlightened?

WHAT'S IT LIKE TO BE
ENLIGHTENED?

To contact Deric or for more information,
visit us at:

www.whatsitliketobeenlightened.com

Made in United States
Orlando, FL
25 August 2022

21519527R00104